THE DOG
THAT WILL CHANGE
YOUR LIFE

Andrew P Pollack

Copyright 2017 by Beachhead Publications, LLC
All rights reserved

ISBN: 978-0-9819477-3-0 print and
ISBN: 978-0-9819477-2-3 e-book

No part of this book may be copied, stored, or transmitted in any form or by any means –without permission of the author, except in the case of brief quotation in critical reviews. The publisher and author are not responsible or liable for any misuse of the material.

For more information, merchandise, or to contact the author:
www.BeachheadPublications.com
or
AndrewPPollack@BeachheadPublications.com

Contents

Chapter One: Doctor 1

Photos: Doctor 11

Chapter Two: Are There Other German Shepherds Like Doctor? Yes! 15

Photos: Stevie 17

Photos: Doctor and Stevie 20

Chapter Three: Selecting a Puppy 23

Photos: Dante 30

Chapter Four: Bringing the Puppy Home 33

Photos: Mr. Cool 52

Epilogue 57

Photos: Karnak 61

About The Author 67

CHAPTER ONE

DOCTOR

This is not a book on how to turn your dog into a well-mannered beast of burden. Read any other book on dog training for that. People like German Shepherd Dogs for the work they can do, but there is much that the public does not know and under appreciates about the soul of a Shepherd.

Much has been written about the German Shepherd as a working dog. This book is about what a wonder a German Shepherd is and how to raise a German Shepherd puppy to help him or her achieve full potential as a companion dog. A German Shepherd Dog, as they are officially known, desires and is capable of being a best friend whose interest is to be involved with 100% of their owner's life and a desire to have the owner be involved in 90% of their life (there are a few things they would rather do by themselves).

Shepherds are imbued with alertness, acute intelligence, communication skills, courage, independence, curiosity, sincerity, tenacity, a full range of emotions, capability for logical reasoned judgment, self-confidence, persistence, fearlessness, a great sense of play, a quick ability to learn, a bond with their owner that cannot be broken, a desire to work, fantastic physical abilities, enthusiasm, and great caring for their owners.

In this world of wars, nuclear threats, rancid politicians, thuggery, violence, insanity, and general low classiness, German Shepherd Dogs (GSD) are a unique gem. Germans Shepherds are known for their heroism. One of the most known early on hero was in

1917 a GSD by the name of Filax of Lewanno was honored at Westminster for bringing 54 wounded soldiers to safety in WW1. During WW1 Germans used the dogs for a variety of purposes. Mercy dogs brought first aid to wounded soldiers after the battle and they would also stay near dying soldiers to keep them company as they (the soldier) passed away. The GSD also delivered messages and worked as guard dogs. There are only three dogs with stars on the Hollywood Walk of Fame, two are GSDs: Strongheart and Rin Tin Tin.

Let me say that I have appreciation for all dog breeds, and have almost never met a dog I didn't like. I think saying my dog is better than your dog is making an odious comparison. However, I have had the privilege of owning German Shepherds for over 45 years, and have developed a great love for the breed. I have seen what a Shepherd can be, and it is a wonder. Shepherds do have communication skills and traits in an amount and combination that is unmatched by other breeds. These abilities may not be attractive to everyone, but for those who appreciate and can relate, there is no substitute. I am writing here about what I know from my own experience not pie in the sky theory. I am going to use "he" for convenience when referring to a Shepherd, but of course everything applies equally to females as well.

The first thing to know about GSDs is that they are capable of so much more than working skills. Most people underestimate the potential of a Shepherd to be a real companion. Quick to want to train them for obedience, the full range of the GSD personality is often ignored and submerged in favor of training them for a particular skill set. Of course, they are not human but have a superior ability to care and be involved with you.

A GSD is a combination of brilliantly assembled genetics and anatomy along with great physical abilities and an individual Being or Spirit that inhabits the body. Just like humans who are a combination of a spiritual non-material Being (sometimes referred to as the Soul or Spirit) and a physical body, so are GSDs. The Being matches flows with the physical universe and so can participate in that time frame. A being that inhabits a dog body is not usually on the same level as a being that inhabits a human body, but a being nonetheless, with capabilities of creation and consideration. Just as you are a unique personality, a non-material entity (whatever the physical universe is made of, you are not made of that), not made of matter or energy or space or time, without wave length or frequency or shape, so is a dog Being. You are a discrete entity capable of opinions, likes, dislikes, and able to make decisions, so is the Being running a dog body although at a lesser level than human Beings. At some point, sometimes before birth, sometimes after birth, the Being joins with the dog body. Without a Being, a dog body or a human body would be no more than a vegetable. Human eyes, ears, noses, or taste buds cannot detect a Spirit or Being because these human senses detect only specific kinds of energy wavelengths. Instruments no matter how delicate can only detect the energy or mass that they were designed to detect. None of this means that you cannot interact and communicate with a Being. At body death, the Being not created of flesh or matter or energy or time as is a body, does not die.

The most basic action in this universe is duplication or copying the environment. Beings do this without analytical thought virtually automatically in an effort to help predict and survive the environment by keeping a record of what to avoid and what to follow. The sheer volume of copies in the course of even one life time comprises a considerable amount of mental energy. Similar energies of a being tend to merge and because this energy is similar to energy that the being is currently putting out the copies can play back against the being. This energy can smother the being's awareness and create irrational responses. The copying of the energy and masses of the physical universe also extends down to the cellular level. Duplication continually in one location or from one viewpoint eventually becomes identification, and thus beings come falsely to believe that they are no more than the energy, masses, and spaces of the physical realm. The same is true for a dog Being.[1]

Unfortunately, in dogs we often recognize only the physical manifestation of life: their bodies and physical skills. There is much more potential in a German shepherd.

I came to my first German Shepherd Dog in the 1970s by accident. My wife wanted a large white dog (a terrible criteria for selecting a dog—you should look for a dog with

---

[1] For a brilliant breakthrough analysis about what life is and the relationship of Beings to the physical universe see the works of Jack Trefaine at: www.Beachheadpublications.com

similar living habits and activity levels to yourself and your family) and when I couldn't find any Huskies, I saw an advertisement in the classifieds for white German Shepherd puppies. I went to see this nice family with seven puppies running around the back yard. They were not professional breeders, but had the litter because they thought it would be fun for their children. There was no genetic or medical history for the mother and father dogs, and it didn't occur to me to ask about this. I am now on my fifth GSD (a four month old puppy) and have learned much from living cheek to jowl with shepherds for the last 45 years.

My first shepherd (the white one) turned out to be a sort of Einstein of dogs, extremely intelligent, very alert, a great communicator, loyal, and full of personality. I named him Doctor, a humorous nod to my mother who always hoped for a professional man in the family (I don't think she ever saw the humor in it).

I worked during the day and at first I put him in a room in the basement with some toys and water. He hated being locked in that room all day and wanted out in the worst way. I figured this out by all the scratches he left on the door. When I came home at night I fed him and played a little ball with him. Eventually he got old enough that I chained him out in the yard all day. I lived in a subdivision of one acre lots that was heavily treed with pines and at that time only built up to the extent of about one house on every five lots. I realized that he didn't like being chained up and after a while I let him run loose all day. This was the 1970s, you could never do this today unless you lived on a ranch or farm. For their own safety dogs need to be in a fenced yard. It turned out that Doctor loved this arrangement, if he couldn't have me to play with all day, he could run around wherever he wanted all day, and he was always there to greet me when I came home.

After about two years, one day I had company over and I went upstairs and Doctor followed me. I didn't really pay much attention, but my guest pointed out that the dog must really like me to follow me around like that. That comment opened my eyes. I should be paying more attention to this creature who wanted to bond more with me.

Up to that time I thought of a dog as more entertainment to me when convenient rather than another being who deserved my attention and respect. Doctor taught me so much of what I know about how GSDs approach problems, communicate, and love to be involved with people. It tuned out that Doctor was an Alpha dog and quickly took to staking out the corners of my lot and defending it from all intruders both human and canine. If a small dog walked on the property, Doctor paid little attention, but if a big dog dared to enter the property he would pick a fight. Somehow he always won. Sometimes he would come home with blood all over him, but it never seemed to be his. For the record I am against all dog fighting, and this is why you need a fenced yard for your dog. On a few occasions when I was present at one of his territorial fights I was foolish enough to reach in and try to grab Doctor's collar and pull him away. Don't try this at home, it is very dangerous to break up a dog fight that way. You can lose a hand.

The 1970s were a different time, and I was young and didn't realize the dangers of letting a dog run loose. Doctor really enjoyed running loose, and he made many friends in the neighborhood. Sometimes the neighbors would invite him into their houses, and on more than one occasion I would be out taking a walk with Doctor on the weekend, and as I walked by a house where children were outside they would call out his name (he had a name tag on his collar). Doctor would trot on over for some stroking. Obviously he had made many friends. Neighborhood kids would sometimes ring my door bell and ask if Doctor could come out and play.

Doctor even had a girlfriend, an Irish setter that lived in the neighborhood. They loved to do things together. They would bark up at chattering squirrels in the trees, or run around together all the time. Two of my other shepherds also found dog companions with whom they really liked to do things. I cannot tell you what their criteria was for close friendship, but they were selective and only chose one such companion.

When I had a date over to the house, I could tell right away if Doctor liked her or not. In the long run his judgment of character was often better than mine, and I would have done well to heed his counsel. I had a wonderful girl friend who really adored Doctor. Whenever she would come to the house, Doctor would hear her car and be at the door when she got there. He would make all kinds of noises in his excitement to see her. She started to make similar noises back. Eventually this encouraged him to speak his mind often. He could modulate his voice and make many different sounds. After a while I could recognize what he was saying and pretty much have a conversation with him. Now I'm not saying I could discuss Shakespeare with him, but after all with how many humans can you have a discussion about Shakespeare? It got so I could have a conservation with him and make out what he was saying.

Recent opining's by scientists say the average dog can recognize 200 words. I don't know how many English words Doctor understood, but it must have been many more. When you communicate to another person or dog there is a carrier wave of intention along with a word sound, and a German Shepherd can pick up on the intention sound or no. A warning here. The more you mimic their sounds the more encouraged they will be to talk. You can end up with a chatterbox. You can communicate quite effectively with your dog and he to you without this.

Usually, Shepherds although they can like many people and consider them all family will tightly bond with only one person, but Doctor was as bonded to that girlfriend as he was to me.

On a few occasions when I broke up with girlfriends, they would ask before they left if they could have custody of Doctor. Of course I never agreed to that, but I can understand why the asked.

It should be remembered that Shepherds are also dogs and like to do dog things, some of which may not be appealing to humans. One time Doctor managed to take a swim in the sewage treatment pond for the subdivision which was about 1/2 mile from my house. I did not enjoy giving him that bath. Dogs must be allowed to be dogs. This points out one of the amazing things about dogs, they are comfortable in the world of man and in the world of dog. I see this as marvelous opportunity to share in both worlds. There are not many species that can exist comfortably in two worlds like that.

Do not underestimate the memory of a German Shepherd. I have seen Doctor immediately recognize a person he had not seen for 6 years (that is 42 years in dog years). All my Shepherds had excellent memories.

Doctor also had reasoned judgment. He was not Pavlovian stimulus-response in his actions. When the doorbell would ring, he ran to the door and would bark until I opened the door. He would keep barking until he saw I was comfortable with the guest.

Protection: There are no other animals and few humans that are willing to jeopardize their own life without a nanosecond of hesitation to protect you like a German Shepherd. Even though I have never needed this type of protection, there is something comforting in knowing that 24 hours a day there is always someone looking out for me.

German Shepherds have two really acute sensing abilities. Their hearing abilities allow them to hear at least four times further than humans, and in a much wider frequency range. They also have an ability to take in a lot of sounds and sort each one out from the rest. They have eighteen muscles in their ears that allow them to position their ears to more directly pick up sounds and to locate the direction from which they are emanating. Friends staying at my house would tell me that Doctor would go to the garage to meet me sometimes as long as a minute before my car started up the driveway. Mr. Cool, my fourth Shepherd could hear me pick up a tee-shirt from any other room in the house even with the TV blasting away or no matter what ambient noises were present. Thinking I was getting dressed to go outside he would immediately show up next to me so he would not miss an opportunity to go along.

Shepherds also have a superior sense of smell which allows them to track smells not only on the ground but in the air. Each nostril can track separately. They have 225 million scent receptors (bloodhounds have even more). Humans have only six million receptors. Their olfactory cortex, which is 40 times bigger than ours, enables them to have superior smelling capabilities. Scientists say that Shepherds can sense between 30,000 to 100,000 different smells, but humans can only sense between 4,000 and 10,000 different smells. Shepherds can smell things up to 40 feet underground and even smell human fingerprints that are a week old. A German Shepherd bites at 238 psi. A human bite is 86 psi.

Because Doctor ran free he built up a musculature that allowed him to operate at peak levels. He was a true athlete. I used to love to see him run. He loved to chase rabbits and squirrels. He never caught one because the rabbits would find a hole or a wood pile to dive into and the squirrels would run up a tree. When guests were over and they saw him running they would always comment on how sleek, fast, and graceful he was. It was truly like watching poetry in motion. Shepherds have superb physical skills that are matched by few other breeds.

Doctor basically raised himself. I was lucky. At least I hadn't forced him into a rigid dog routine or stifled his personality by making him live in a small crate and demanding a very limited behavior or training routine with no human understanding. I always treated him with respect.

Voted the number one dog for loyalty, GSDs offer loyalty to the nines. Their loyalty implies a faithfulness that is steadfast in the face of any temptation to renounce, desert, or betray. They never sell out to the other side. This attractive quality seems to have been mostly lost in 21st century society with its every man for self-gain, but not in German Shepherds.

I can't take a lot of the credit for creating Doctor as a highly evolved personality, but I never stifled his being. I let him be what he could be. Of course, especially when in the house or with me outside he had to obey certain rules, but he was happy to do so as he realized I returned his loyalty, respected him greatly and wanted him to prosper and be happy.

By observation, Doctor basically taught me what a Shepherd could be. I learned more from my later Shepherd companions on how to encourage the great potential in a German shepherd.

When Doctor was about five years old my business required that I travel for days at a time. I would have someone come over and feed him, and he had a dog door so he could go into the house whenever he wanted. I thought he must get bored and lonely so I decided he might like another shepherd for company. I looked around locally and just happened to find a litter of all black Shepherds available. I picked out a female I named Stevie (no, not inspired by Stevie Nicks, but by a television show character) and brought her home to be with Doctor. I thought this would be true harmony for the dogs let alone the nice symbolism of black and white living together.

This was a huge mistake. Doctor was not interested in puppy behavior. Being a puppy, Stevie butted in on everything I would do with Doctor. Whenever I was petting Doctor, she would stick her nose into the action. For at least a year I am sure Doctor thought I got Stevie to punish him in some way. But eventually when Stevie got over the puppy stage, she became a very well mannered, sweet tempered dog. From this I learned that puppies will learn from older dogs. In fact this is a great way to teach behavior to a puppy.

Stevie turned out to be perfectly mannered in an elegant and dignified lady like way. Unlike most dogs who might shadow you or get under your feet or get right in front of you, if you were going upstairs Stevie would walk along side of you in lock step. She acted as if she were waiting for your command without you having to instruct her. She was content just to be in your company. Stevie always carried herself with a regal air.

Doctor and Stevie both lived to between 12 and 13 years old. The average life span for a wolf in the wild is 5 years. The average lifespan for a domesticated German Shepherd is around 11 years. This illustrates what I think is the major flaw in German Shepherds. They should have a life span equal to their owner's. What mostly seems to wear out in Shepherds is their hind end. Their hearts stay strong, their minds are still sharp, their will never diminishes. It is usually their back legs or spine that fails in some way. Perhaps this is the price for having such a fine tuned high performance body, it just burns out early from such extreme use.

When Doctor was close to 13 years old his back legs finally wouldn't work for him, and he could no longer walk. I had seen this coming for some time and it greatly saddened me, but in line with my personal philosophy which I want applied to myself when I no longer have quality of life and there is no hope for recovery, I knew it was time to have him euthanized and released from a body that was no longer serving him well. There comes a time in every dog's life when this decision has to be made. This is a personal decision and each owner must decide for himself.

I explained to Doctor that although it pained me greatly to loose contact with him, it was an opportunity for him to get a new body that would allow him to express himself in the expansive manner that was worthy of him. When you have a talk with your dog about philosophical subjects you are often not sure how much they comprehend, but I feel that it is better to have a conversation than not have one.

The next day with tears in my eyes I carried him into the car and made the drive to the veterinarian's office for our appointment. Often a veterinarian will just take the dog into the back room and do the job, but I feel I owe it to my friend to be with him to the end. Having now been through this four times I can tell you that it is always a very sad and difficult. There comes a time in every dog's life when this decision has to be made.

After I left the veterinarian's office I drove to the beach to take a walk along the ocean before going to work. I had this odd feeling and then I realized that the Being of Doctor was still with me. We had been so close for so long that he didn't want to leave my space and time. I knew he needed to carry on and told him so. I could sense him leaving, and I suddenly felt better. Of course to this day when I think about him I still miss him, but I feel good that wherever he is he is having a life that he can enjoy fully as a proud German Shepherd.

Doctor as pup-tail proudly high

Doctor running thru wild flowers

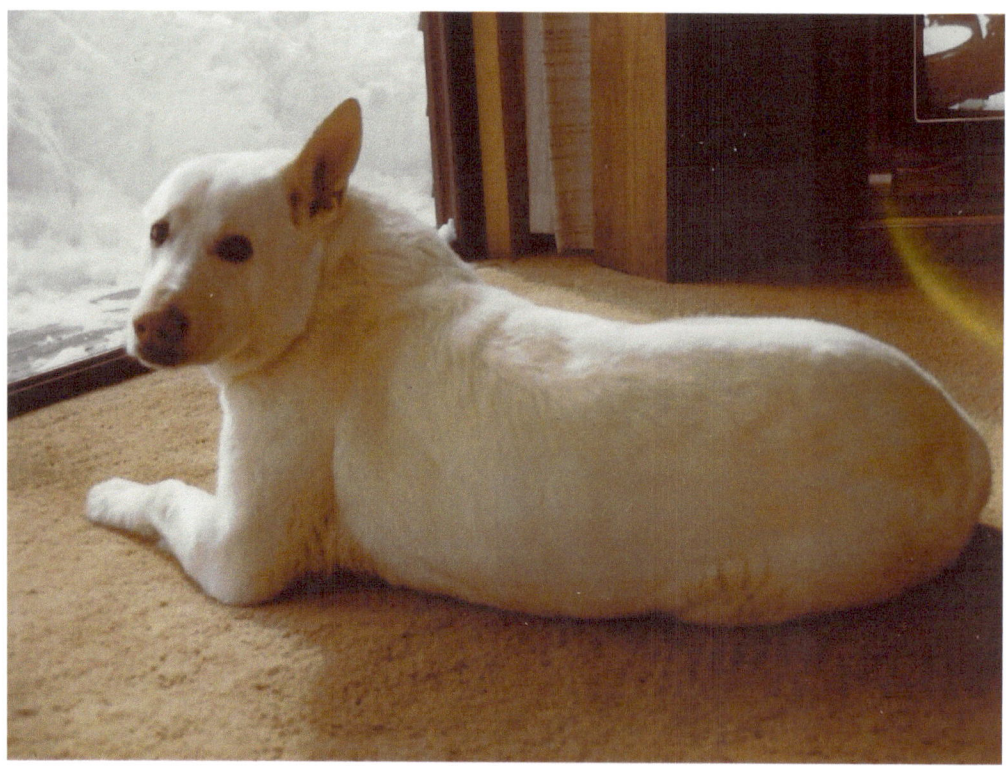
Doctor checking out snow

Doctor in snow

Doctor lounging in back yard

Doctor after bath

Doctor playing with ball

Doctor checking things out on fishing trip

CHAPTER TWO

ARE THERE OTHER GERMAN SHEPHERDS LIKE DOCTOR? YES!

By this time you are probably saying that Doctor was exceptional even for a German Shepherd. Well, maybe not. Of course, like people all Shepherds are not the same. I am quite certain that the potential for high level intelligence and understanding exists in all German Shepherds. It is a matter of not suppressing but rather encouraging and allowing these higher level traits to germinate and expand. A good general guide line standard for German Shepherds is the "SV" standard originally set up by Max Von Stephanitz (the "inventor" of the German shepherd)[2].

I have owned three other Shepherds after Doctor and Stevie: Dante, Mr. Cool, and now Karnak, a four month old puppy. I have learned from and been impressed by each of them. More on this later.

Most importantly each one has an individual and unique Being running the dog body. You do not get a blank slate with each puppy that you can mold into whatever you want. What happens most often with Shepherds is that they are used as work animals. Taught to do a specific task, with little or no attention to the higher traits that are available. Shepherd bodies copy and identify with what they are taught in a way that allows humans to harness some of their great physical skills like sense of smell or hearing and alertness. This kind of intense training often subsumes much of a Shepherds' personality.

---

[2] http://www.germanshepherdguide.com/the-german-sv-standard.html

Training practices that use Shepherds like dumb animals have hurt the genetic lines. There have been and no doubt still are great abuses. Does anyone think training a German Shepherd to patrol concentration camps during the 1930s and 1940s in Germany was good for the dogs. Did the Russians in WWII, Pol Pot's regime during the 1970s, or today's North Koreans treat their dogs well? Although our military has improved the conditions for their dogs considerably, they are still used as a disposable machine. Police departments that train a dog to attack should never be allowed to so. Do we need to twist a dog's natural inclination to befriend humans into encouraging dogs to attack humans? All of this hurts not only the dogs so used, but also harms the entire genetic line and Spirits of the species. Remember duplication is the most basic action of life and copies are so retained as psychic energy as well as in the cells and genetic lines.

Estimates are all over the place on this (I guess some of those pesky dogs won't return the census forms), but a fair estimate is that there are 600,000,000 dogs in the world and only 223,000,000 are pets. That leaves 377,000,000 feral dogs with no health care or predictable food to eat left to forage for themselves in garbage dumps and in the wild. There are many great animal welfare organizations in the industrialized world, but much is left to be done to improve the lot of dogs. After these depressing statistics, let us return to what you and I can effectively do to improve a dog's and our lives.

Stevie as puppy

Stevie on walk in Colorado

Stevie relaxing on walk at Lake Tahoe

Stevie on walk on California coast

Stevie at my Mother's house enjoying the holiday cheer

A 12 year old Stevie

Stevie with Doctor in foreground

Doctor and Stevie in back yard

Doctor and Stevie relaxing

Doctor and Stevie in Montana

Doctor and Stevie in Motel in Wyoming

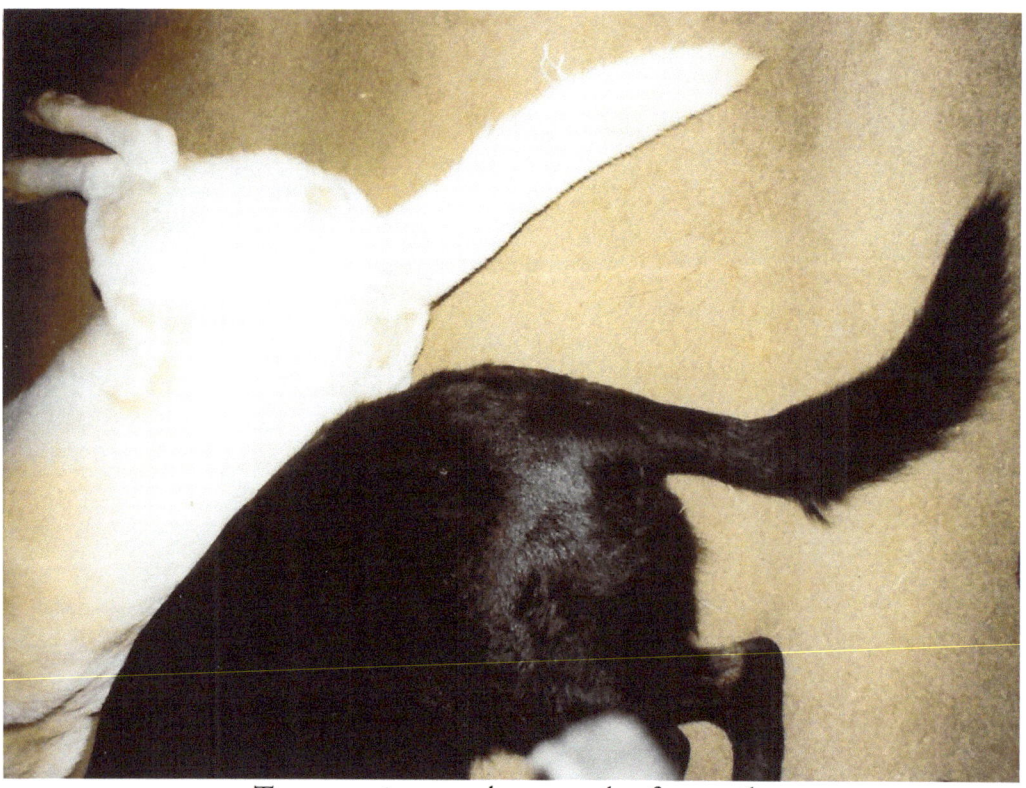
Two snoozing pooches— a tale of two tails

CHAPTER THREE

SELECTING A PUPPY

Quite a few books have been written on how to select a puppy. Good German shepherd puppies are hard to come by and in my opinion there are not many great breeders. A good puppy should come from a genetic line tested for hip dysplasia, and the most recent scourge of careless breeding, Degenerative Myelopathy. There is a central clearing house for certifying German Shepherd hips in Missouri.[3] Veterinarians can take X-rays to be sent there for evaluation. There is now an inexpensive accurate test for DM. My fourth shepherd, Mr. Cool succumbed to this awful disease at 10 years old. It is a progressive disease of the spinal cord outer sheathing breaking down. The dogs lose control of their hind legs. It often does not show any signs until the dog is around 6 to 8 years of age. Currently there are no treatments or cures. Often after the visible symptoms appear, within six months the dog has lost his ability to walk. Mr. Cool willed himself to compensate with his front legs for more than a year. I would put booties on his back feet so when they dragged he would not scrape the skin off his feet. He loved taking his daily walk and seeing his girlfriend so much that he compensated with increased strength and muscle tone in his front legs, but eventually even he could walk no more. I still miss him.

There is a very valuable lesson that can be learned from Mr. Cool's illness. When German Shepherds have a disability or injury, they do not sit around and feel sorry for themselves. Their thoughts are not consumed on how this will affect their lives. They just adjust as best they can and go on with life. I have seen this with a number of my animals. It is a good lesson for humans.

---

[3] ORTHOPEDIC FOUNDATION FOR ANIMALS HTTP://WWW.OFA.ORG/INDEX.HTML

A note here on dog health. Dogs like humans do not have perfect bodies. During the lifetime of any dog or human there will be some disease or defect that needs treatment. You just have to accept this and be prepared to have a good veterinarian treat your friend. I have been through a tonsillectomy (when the vet first suggested that Doctor needed to have his tonsils out I thought he was joking), but it cured Doctor's constant coughing.

Stevie had two gastric torsions. This is where too much air and gas in the chest cavity can cause the stomach to flip strangling the windpipe and if not corrected immediately by surgery will be fatal. The first one was not corrected properly by surgery and so it re-occurred. The second time it was.

My one really bad experience with a veterinarian was when my third Shepherd, Dante, tore a cranial cruciate ligament at his knee. After a number of consultations I agreed to have some orthopedic veterinarians operate. I made an appointment for the surgery. When I showed up for the appointment, the receptionist had no record of the surgery. This should have been a big red flag to me, but I just made another appointment. When I came to pick up Dante after surgery they couldn't even find him at first. They had told me that he would be watched 24 hours a day through the two day recovery period. They botched the job and Dante was in terrible pain for the rest of his life. When I took him back in for a follow up they just made a bunch of excuses. The cost was something like $3,800.00 back in 2005 which they made me pay up front (another warning sign). At the time I was actually comforted by the high fee as I thought to charge this much these orthopedic veterinarians must be good. I was wrong. It turned out they were running a money mill and were more interested in profits than the dogs they treated. My natural inclination (and probably yours) is to assume that anyone dealing with animals cares about the animal's welfare and that their priorities would be to do whatever was necessary to ensure the animal came first; sadly, this is not always true with all breeders or all veterinarians. You must do as much research as you can on the people with whom you entrust the care of your pet. I had consulted with my local vet and had a consultation with a professor from the University of Missouri College of Veterinary Medicine who both recommended the procedure. I am sure they both had good intentions, but they did not know the surgeons. Remember you are dealing with humans who can all make mistakes. One of the good aspects of the internet is that you can do your own research on dog health issues. I always feel that in the final analysis with the welfare of my dog, the buck stops with me.

At four years old Mr. Cool suddenly developed an abscess on his neck. My veterinarian operated and cut out the abscess. The lab results were that it was cancerous. I treated him as I would want for myself in a similar situation and did not pursue oncology which I thought would torture him. He healed quickly and lived another 6 years without a re-occurrence of the cancer. These types of decisions are personal and each owner has to decide what he or she thinks is right for the animal.

Karnak has already required surgery to have a broke n baby tooth extracted to protect the adult tooth from getting infected. I asked a lot of questions of the veterinarian before I agreed. Questions like: "How many of these procedures have you done?", "How many had serious complications?", "What scientific studies validate your theory of why the procedure was necessary?" Even though he could not cite any study that showed that removing a broken baby tooth would avoid contamination to an adult tooth, to my veterinarian's credit he answered every question honestly. In the end I went with his experience. The tooth extraction was successful.

There are two points to this. First, not all veterinarians are of equal skill. Everyone wants to think his personal doctor went to Harvard Medical School and was at the top of the class. But there are many C minus and D students out there in both human medicine and dog medicine. The average veterinarian is like a country general practitioner. Some are more skilled than others and some as in any profession just have a knack for their work. There are now more and more specialists in areas of veterinary medicine. I am not concerned as much as to where a veterinarian went to school as much as I care about his or her attentiveness for animals and his or her experience. This particularly applies to any non-emergency elective procedure. There are always risks in any surgery especially with anesthesia. There is still a fair portion of human and veterinary medicine based on "everyone knows" rather than rigorous scientific research. There is much that medicine does not yet know about human or dog bodies.

One more note, yes, veterinarians have gotten expensive. They have all gone to conferences where they attend lectures on how to create profit centers in their practice. I believe veterinarians are entitled to makes a good living if they deliver good quality services. Be prepared to spend some money on your friend. There are now a number of pet insurance companies. I have not seen reliable research as to whether this is a good value or not, so I will not opine on the value of pet insurance. Although I maintain insurance for my car, house, and health, I do not like the concept of insurance as I do not like to bet against myself. When you think about it, you are paying for insurance because you think something bad will happen to you. That is betting against yourself. I like to be more positive in my attitude. Insurance is a personal decision for each dog owner to decide. My viewpoint is this: If you take a few thousand dollars in dog health costs and divide it amongst the number of days in an average Shepherd life of 11 years, it amounts only to pennies a day. Whatever you spend on your dog, it is the best buy you can ever make in entertainment, love, and friendship.

Back to selecting a puppy. I have a few simple rules. Most importantly you want the sire and dam to be on site where you can interact with them. Are they friendly? Do they seem happy? If the breeder won't let you interact with both parents for any reason, this is a huge warning sign.

Pick up and hold the puppy. Does he seem content with you holding him? If he or she tries to bite you, this is not the puppy for you.

The puppy should be active, no discharges, have clear eyes, and good teeth.

Veterinarians and many breeders will tell you that females are more protective than males. My limited only one experience with a female (Stevie) did not follow this pattern at all. Stevie was the sweetest, most friendly, and well behaved Shepherd you could find. If someone rang the doorbell, she would bark once or twice then line up at the door to give every stranger a kiss. This might be because she was raised with Doctor who was an alpha male and always looked out for her so she never had to be on protection duty. I think the individual personality is much more telling than the sex in predicting how a German Shepherd will behave. My experience is that both females and males can make great companions.

Your contract with the breeder should allow you ten days to have your veterinarian examine the puppy and give you the right to return him for any reason for a full refund in that time period.

It is possible but not likely that you will develop an immediate bond on the spot with a puppy. You have to realize that you can't know everything about a puppy's personality or future health on the spot. There are certain unknowns when meeting a puppy, but by doing the above you get the odds in your favor for selecting a great healthy friend.

Remember all puppies are cute. This proves nothing. My theory is that whoever invented dogs made puppies cute so you wouldn't strangle them when they tear up your house.

As a practical matter German Shepherd Dogs have a number of distinct lineages you can choose from. Schutzhund lines, East German lines, European lines, and American lines.

Schutzhund means Protection Dog in German. The Germans take their Shepherds very seriously. Schutzhund dogs are trained for obedience, tracking, and protection. The Bunderssieger Zuchtschau is held every year in Germany. German Shepherds from all over the world come to compete. There are often more than 40,000 spectators for the event. It is like the Kentucky Derby for German Shepherd Dogs. I find that Schutzhund dogs are bred for their drive and are sometimes better as working dogs than companions, but there are always exceptions, and it depends on with whom they are bred.

Karnak's grandfather, Zamp vom Thermados was a very popular world champion in 2006, often referred to as Zamp the Legend. He turned out to have great physical skills and a very friendly and charismatic personality. There are still many articles and photos of Zamp on the web. Zamp's owner, young Lisa Dieterich was only 8 years old when Zamp was born, nonetheless it was she who picked him out from the litter, Lisa has often recounted that, "when he was young he was a no good dog, very long and croup was not good also". When asked why she chose Zamp as a puppy, she replied, "I just loved him the most because he was the one who was fat and always wanted to sleep"[4]. No one can tell exactly how a puppy will turnout.

There are no doubt hundreds of Zamp decedents out there. I didn't go looking for a descendant of a world champ and I would not recommend any one else do so either. Much depends on both parents and the nurturing environment. Lineage is important but does not guarantee all that much about personality. When I saw Karnak he was fairly calm so I did not worry about too much drive.

Eastern European shepherds are especially developed in USSR for military, guarding or guiding, not as good for companions.

King Shepherds are bred for their very large size. They often have health problems. Stay away.

American lines. All lines descend from German lines, but I prefer dogs bred in the United States. My favorite state for Shepherds is Colorado. Doctor, Stevie, and Karnak came from Colorado, but I wouldn't limit myself to Colorado shepherds.

Mr. Cool and Dante came from California. They were all great dogs. I am sure there are good breeders in almost every state.

You will see many ads and websites promoting Shepherds imported from Europe. This is not a good way to secure a companion dog. You will really know nothing but what you are told about the parents which may or may not be true. Imported dogs are also more expensive.

A word about the American Kennel Club (AKC). Most people have seen on TV the

---

[4] http://konkurrenzloskennel.blogspot.com/2017/01/get-to-know-our-gsds-part-iii-sandro.html

Westminster Kennel Club Dog Show. This the United States world championship for AKC dogs. It's a beauty contest; the only thing missing are questions for the entrants about world peace. To qualify as an AKC purebred a dog must meet a list of arbitrary physical requirements.[5]

Mr. Cool came from a breeder who placed her dogs in shows all over California. According to the AKC standards for show, no white is allowed on a German shepherd's paws. Mr. Cool had white coloring on his paws and since the breeder could not show him they were willing to sell him to me. There is fashion in everything and AKC dogs are no exception. Fashion also explains why every few years I go into my closet and get out the wide or narrow ties depending on what is in fashion. In the case of Mr. Cool this was a break for me as I had spent months trying to locate a breeder in California where I was living who would sell me a dog. Nevertheless, fashionable appearance is a dumb way to evaluate a companion dog. Neither Mr. Cool nor I ever cared a whit about the color of his feet.

With AKC it is all about appearance. I do not think this is a good way to select a dog. Besides does anyone really think that the appearance that you like, other dogs recognize? Are dogs attracted to another dog that meets the AKC requirements? Do dogs pick their friends based on appearance? Do they like you because of your appearance? Take a lesson from the dog world. Appearance is the least valuable way to pick a companion dog.

My suggestions are to investigate the breeder. Are there any complaints against them? Are they properly licensed? Check with the state animal bureau. Google the breeder's name. All this can be done on line in a few minutes. It doesn't guarantee anything, but it might show someone to avoid.

I have found that good breeders are very happy to talk with you at length on the phone and tell you all about their lines and what is their philosophy on dogs. I like breeders whose puppies have lots of interaction with humans and preferably live in the house with their human family. Good breeders are very proud of their animals.

---

[5] You can download the appearance requirements for a German Shepherd from this site: https://cdn.akc.org/GermanShepherdDog.pdf

Dante at 1 year

Dante on walk on California central coast

Dante running thru wild flowers in Colorado

Dante checking out overlook in Oregon

Dante sleeping on couch

Dante relaxing after busy day on California central coast

CHAPTER FOUR

BRINGING THE PUPPY HOME

I am going to say something here that is probably politically incorrect. I confess that I really don't care all that much for puppies. They are constantly getting into things, testing your will, and, oh, that nasty period before they are housebroken. But since I love and adore adult Shepherds, puppydom is something you have to endure all the while taking great care of and interacting with your puppy guiding him to be the fantastic adult he can be. Expect to be exasperated over and over, it is worth the efforts you need to put in to nurture him to adulthood.

After Stevie passed away, I wanted another Shepherd and an advertisement appeared in the classifieds for a GSD with very good lineage that was 1 year old. I thought this would be a great way to obtain another Shepherd without the hassles of putting up with a puppy. Dante's owner worked 12 hour days, didn't know much about raising dogs and had locked him up for 15 hours or more a day in a crate. When I met Dante he was cautious but pleasant. I am sure he was glad to get out of the crate. I noticed this but thought that after a while with me he would get over any anxieties he had, and we did bond well and had many good times. However, he never got over his suspicion of humans. German Shepherds are very strong willed, and if they feel that something is bad for their survival they will not let go of that idea easily. He would growl at people we saw on walks, and often snap at them, was never good in crowds, and was never as happy as my other dogs. I could never get him over this. I learned from this that the first year especially is very influential on a German Shepherd's personality.

One time Dante saved me from a burglar. He was barking a lot and when I looked out I saw a person fleeing from my garage. When you have a German Shepherd with his loud and deep bark, any burglar will decide to skip your house and find another without a GSD on duty. For my money a Shepherd is better than any alarm system or burglar alarm company.

I want to say that people who rescue dogs and adopt them from shelters are doing a great service. I applaud and commend them. This is good for people, and this is good for dogs. However, the safest way to ensure that your German Shepherd friend will be happy and live up to its full potential is to get him as a puppy.

A puppy is just getting used to this world and his new body. He is trying to establish his place and his reach into the environment. On top of this his body is growing at an outstanding rate. At birth a German shepherd puppy is deaf and blind. Karnak weighed 1 lb at birth. At eight weeks when I picked him up he weighed 10 pounds, and at four months he weighed 38 lb. A lot is going on with their bodies including hormones flowing, and I am sure this influences how they act.

Like all Beings entering a new environment German Shepherds will reach out to see what effects they can create and then withdraw. Each time they will reach out a little further to test their abilities. This often leads to mischief and destruction, but if handled correctly they will learn the limitations that you require for a happy shared living space.

Just like with human babies, sensations for a puppy are magnified and sharper than in an adult; so expect that at times a puppy will be strongly stimulated. They are testing out their bodies, how fast can they run, jump, and chew things. This is natural. Know that they will aggravate and stress you in their forays into the environment. You must not panic or harshly punish them for these activities. Your patience will be tested. Expect it.

Prepare your home as much as possible by removing items close to the floor that a puppy might like to chew on. Remove any low level electric wires or anything that can be reached by a puppy. Keep in mind that every week as he grows he will be able to reach a little higher.

Get them some toys of their own. Regarding dog toys, do no give them hard surface toys. They can break their own baby teeth if they are heavy chewers. Think of it this way: would you chew on a ceramic bone? Don't give them anything that you wouldn't have your teeth chew on.

I believe that the best time to pick up a Shepherd puppy is at 8 to 12 weeks old. Eight weeks is ideal.

A note on food. It now seems like everybody from TV personalities to Ma and Pa Kettle and his cousin has a dog food on the market. I'm surprised Justin Bieber and Katy Perry don't have one. You need to do research on this and consult with your veterinarian. I wouldn't rely solely on the advice of your veterinarian however. There is much misinformation and advertising that is misleading on this subject. Dry food is much easier to use and less expensive than canned food. There are some very good dry dog foods on the market. There are some made explicitly for German Shepherds.

For two reasons I recommend that you do not give your dog table scraps or human food. Once you establish this it quickly becomes an expectation and you can have a dog that looks for food on your kitchen counters (counter surfing) or begs for it at meal time. Human food is not nutritionally balanced for a dog as dog food is and tends to be too high in fat. Keeping your Shepherd lean will avoid extra stress on his hind quarters.

I would avoid dog food made in China. There have been instances of pet deaths from chemicals in Chinese made dog food. We just don't know if they adhere to high enough quality standards.

You want a puppy chow that is made for large dogs. These contain important nutrients that a large breed like German Shepherds need during their growth period. There is even a dog food made for German Shepherd puppies. With German Shepherds this puppy food should be fed until about 15 months when you can change over to adult food. Selecting a high quality dog chow ensures that your dog will have fewer health problems during his life.

A lot of data is available on the web, but who knows if it is well researched or just advertising masquerading as real science. I also assume that dog food companies sponsor events for Veterinarians like drug companies do for human doctors, and feed the doctor only positive data on their products. Pharmaceutical companies are taking a growing interest in animal care. This will be good news for dogs as more research is done and new drugs are produced. Sales of vaccines, medicines and medical devices for companion animals now exceed about $8 billion annually. However as money can sometimes bring a corrupting influence, pet owners should inform themselves and question excesses. There was a recent study with doctors for humans that showed that the bigger the gifts to doctors from drugs companies, the greater the number of prescriptions the doctors wrote.[6]

Mr. Cool, the most protective of all my shepherds, had eating issues from the day I got him. At first I thought it was just a puppy thing that would pass. I called the breeder for tips but they wouldn't return my calls so I assume the breeder knew about this problem. Mr. Cool was a very finicky eater and would often have bouts of diarrhea. I took him to the veterinarian who suspected exocrine pancreatic insufficiency, or EPI which is occurring more commonly in German Shepherds, but this was not the case for Mr. Cool. EPI, hip dysplasia and degenerative myelopathy are diseases that better breeding practices could mostly eliminate. Every breed has a list of diseases that they are prone to because of bad breeding. Medical problems from poor breeding are on the rise.[7]

The Vet did numerous tests but could never come up with more than a generic name of IBT (Irritable Bowel Syndrome) that meant little more than stomach upset. Human doctors do this too. Providing no solutions they feel that if they give a body problem a name they have earned their fee. Whatever happened to paying people based on results? Workers in the field are paid by the piece, but the higher up the money chain you go

---

[6] https://www.nytimes.com/2017/10/25/well/live/the-more-lavish-the-gifts-to-doctors-the-costlier-the-drugs-they-prescribe.html?rref=collection%2Fsectioncollection%2Fhealth&action=click&contentCollection=health&region=stream&module=stream_unit&version=latest&contentPlacement=8&pgtype=sectionfront&_r=0

[7] http://www.hsvma.org/assets/pdfs/guide-to-congenital-and-heritable-disorders.pdf

the less compensation is tied to results. There appears to be less and less accountability high on the employment chain. All too often we have an abundance of crony capitalism, and as my grandfather used to say: "we have the finest politicians money can buy".

I must have tried 20 different dog foods in an attempt to find a food Mr. Cool could tolerate. After a few years I finally came upon a frozen food that was made from naturally raised chickens and vegetables freshly cooked and then frozen. It came in 1 lb containers, and Mr. Cool consumed three a day at a cost of around $20 a day. This settled all his stomach problems. To me this dog was worth it, but paying $7,000 a year for dog food is not a situation you will enjoy. Mr. Cool was a terrific companion and I considered him a priceless friend.

Mr. Cool was a very friendly dog and liked people and other dogs. One of his good dog pals was a Chihuahua. He would see her quite often when out walking and the first thing when they met was they would give each other a big kiss. To me it was funny sight to see this tiny dog and this big dog playing together. He had very large feet and his front paws had white coloring making them look even bigger. Some of my neighbors would refer to him as Big Foot. When they saw him they would call out: "Hey Big Foot, come over and say hello", and he would. He was extremely protective of me, a trait I did not teach him or encourage, but was enhanced by his own feelings toward me. I had a desk in my house and unless he knew a person extremely well when they approached the desk he would let out a few barks and hover around to let them know he was on the job. His loyalty to me was boundless.

Don't be surprised if your puppy throws up on the ride home. The pup has probably never been in a car before. They get over this fairly quickly. I had to make a five hour drive to get Karnak, and sure enough on the way home he threw up in the first 10 minutes, but after he threw up the rest of the trip was uneventful. Take your pup on rides often and he will soon learn to like going with you.

Let's talk crates. I do not care for crates, especially for a large dog like a German Shepherd. It is too small a space, very confining for a puppy. I know you can find a lot of data about crate training, but would you like to be confined to a small space where you could not move around? Remember my experience with Dante.

There needs to be a space where you can confine a puppy. I recommend what is called an Exercise Pen. They come up to 48" in height and are a wire enclosure with no top, about 3 foot by 4 foot in size and the puppy can see out of all sides and can move around. They are available from Amazon and elsewhere on the internet and cost about $60.

I put a water dish in the enclosure, some bedding, and always feed the pup in there so that he has a positive attitude toward the pen. Place the pen near where your family's activities take place so that they don't feel abandoned and alone. This is where a puppy should sleep at night at least until he is house broken.

You need a well fenced yard for the dog to go outside. It doesn't have to be huge but big enough for a dog to run around. German Shepherds are moderately active canines and like exercise and play, but will not demand perpetual action. Well cared for German Shepherds are basically homebodies and not likely to run away, but a good fence is also important for keeping other creatures out.

Although this will not work for everyone, here is a practical tip on yards. I used to have natural grass in my yard. I was always having it re-sodded or re-seeded. Weather, dog digging, and sprinkler mishaps often caused my grass to have patches that were dead and soon became exposed dirt. When it rained or after watering this turned to mud, and when the dogs came into the house they had muddy feet if not dirt on their coats. Then I discovered artificial turf. I replaced my grass with artificial turf that was low-slip and bacterial resistant. Many water districts will even pay you to remove water guzzling grass. I am now on my third dog to use this grass and they have all been very happy with it. It is easy to clean up after the dogs do their business on it, the dog's feet and their bodies stay cleaner much longer, and my water bill is lower. I also xeriscaped my flower beds by putting down a moisture barrier, then top soil, and then medium size rock to retain the moisture. This eliminated any exposed dirt. The plants and trees did well too.

One nice thing about German Shepherds is that their hair does not need trimming, and they do not require costly trips to the dog groomer. I just put my Shepherds into the bath tub (use only shampoo made for dogs) and give them a bath every two months or so. Shepherds do not have a body odor.

All German Shepherds shed some of their fur. If they spend a lot of time outside in a cold climate they will grow a very thick coat in winter, but they will shed heavily in spring and summer. The best way to minimize shedding is to brush the dog regularly. Baths get rid of the body oils that make dead hair cling to the dog. My dogs have all liked being brushed.

I believe one of the most valuable inventions of all time is the dog door. I think it is right up there with the personal computer, the cell phone, and the car. You don't have to have one, but it is a godsend for you and the pup. The dog can go out and do his business any time of day or night, and you don't have to think about his outdoor needs. Be sure to get one big enough for an adult Shepherd. If you have trouble finding wall space to install one, you can get a custom installation in a glass sliding door. German Shepherds seem to have an amazing ability to hold it in, but why torture the poor guy. I know when I gotta go, I gotta go.

A word about neighbors. Your Shepherd will bark at times. You need to make sure that your neighbors are ok with this. Many years ago somebody threw a small ball into my yard. It could have been from the street side even though the walls are 6 foot high. Dante swallowed the ball and it disturbed his digestive system. When an object showed on an x-ray, the veterinarian recommended that it be surgically removed. After surgery when the veterinarian showed me the ball I was shocked, knowing that I had left no such item in my yard. Was it some neighbor? Someone passing by? I will never know. My current neighbors on both sides and behind me all have dogs of their own, and I do not have this worry. I don't mind when their dogs bark and they don't mind when my dogs bark, but if Mr. Cool got carried away with barking over something I was quick to bring him inside to make sure he was not irritating the neighbors, especially late at night. Better to be safe than sorry. Canines are sometimes more trustworthy than humans and certainly less cruel.

If you go away on a trip and leave your German shepherd at home, it is likely that at night he will go outside and howl like a wolf would howl at the moon. He misses you and wants everyone to know how much. The neighbors will not appreciate this. When away keep dogs inside at night to avoid this problem.

Not let's get down to what is really important. How you should relate to the puppy.

From my 45 years of dog ownership, I have gained respect for German Shepherds.

No, make that tremendous respect. Even for a puppy I immediately have respect knowing what he or she will be. I don't think of them as a lesser life form. Sure, they are not human, but in some ways superior to many humans. My respect on some level immediately communicates to the puppy, and a pup will rise to meet this. If you have low expectations for your canine, he or she will often not rise to best potential. Expectations often become reality.

Having respect immediately sets a standard of interaction, and the dogs pick this up. Maybe it is just a little application of The Golden Rule. I don't expect them to do a calculous problem or figure the Internal Rate of Return of an investment, but don't we already have enough people doing those things. Is the world in such great shape because of it? I respect Shepherds for how they live their lives with integrity, consistency of thought, and their caring for humans. On some level Shepherds accept my expectations and it becomes mutual respect. This doesn't mean that the puppy won't aggravate you by urinating on your rug or chewing up a favorite magazine you left within his reach. Their genetics dictate this type of behavior.

Whenever my dog enters the room I am in I always acknowledge his presence. Just say "Hey buddy", or "What's Doing", or any other greeting. Not to acknowledge his existence is an invalidation of his Being. The same principle applies to humans. Everybody had a school teacher that belittled or ignored them. Did this feel good?

For puppies I like to give them some pets whenever they come in from outside, just so they know that I am happy to see them.

Discipline. All children and dogs at times need some discipline. All organization and rules to some degree limit individual freedom, but in order to share space in a sane way with others we need to have some rules and boundaries. Puppies also need to know there are procedures, rules, and life styles that must be observed.

Rule #1. **Never hit your dog.**
Rule #2. **Never kick your dog.**

If you train a German Shepherd with physical punishment, you cannot count on his loyalty. Whereas if you train a GSD with positive reinforcement, nothing can ever break the bond of loyalty to you, and he will want to do as you ask. This is not immediately apparent in puppies, but over time with correct training you can count on him to want to work with you on any subject. The same is true for humans. Those made to modify their behavior by bullying or forced means will be looking for a way to revolt. Once you have gained a Shepherd's loyalty, neither fear nor punishment can prevent him from going all out up to and including sacrificing his own life on your behalf.

German Shepherds respect strength once they see your leadership skills, but it must be done with kindness. You need to show that you are the boss. This is best done with your demeanor and verbal tone. When you want to communicate with your dog about some unacceptable behavior, verbally reprimand him firmly. The most important aspect of correcting bad behavior is patience and firmness. Keep in mind that their DNA was programmed to make them push restlessly out into the environment to help them survive in the wild. At the puppy stage they are overwhelmed with the sensations from their new bodies but their brains are not fully formed, thus they are unable to balance out instincts with logic. The brain was designed to give the Being control of his body, but puppy brains are small. At eight weeks when I picked up Karnak like all puppies of his age his skull was very small but grew at a very fast rate to accommodate the growth fulfillment of the brain. Once the skull reaches full size the brain has room to complete its complex nervous systems. Studies in humans show that a child's brain undergoes an amazing period of development from birth to three, producing more than a million neural connections each second. I am unaware of brain studies in animals but it is likely that there is also great growth in dog brains over a lifetime, so be a little patient with your puppy.

Do not get riled up or respond excitedly to their activities. German Shepherds puppies are testing their ability to create effects and to get you involved. Let me repeat that: they want to get you involved; this makes a better game. With bad behavior if you react excitedly, you will just be encouraging and prolonging the game. A calm but very firm 'No" is the right way to go. Appeal to their intelligence not to their wildness. Don't expect immediate acquiescence to your will, however. You will be rewarded for your time and patience one hundred times over when the pup matures.

It is tempting to just put them in a kennel or outside and leave them there. There will be times when this is necessary for a cooling off period. However, the more time you spend with your puppy the greater the bond you will create, and the greater intelligence and understanding of you he will have.[8]

Puppies like two year old humans are not always rational in their behavior. You can expect that there will be times when you will be exasperated with how they respond I sometimes use a small spray bottle (such as used for plant misting) and fill it with **water only**, set the pray to heavy mist, and give the pup a spray when he is doing something antisocial. Puppies don't like this, but it does them no real harm. They will get the message after a few sprays. I have also rolled up sheets of newspaper and hit my palm or another hard object (not the dog). This produces a sound that puppies don't like. Often I just put the puppy out in the yard for a "time out".

Remember when you get a puppy or a human baby you do not get a blank slate on which you can write whatever you want. Environment and nurture are also very influential, but not the whole story. There is a real live Being there likely with previous life experiences. When I picked up Mr. Cool he was 10 weeks old, and had never seen a veterinarian. He was very friendly with all the people that came to my house or that he would meet on his walks. The first time I took him to a veterinarian, the whole time he was there he barked wildly and was literally screaming, and trying his utmost to stay

---

[8] https://www.psychologytoday.com/blog/canine-corner/200811/building-better-brain-your-dog

away from the Vet. My Vet was very good with animals, but Mr. Cool would bark and try as hard as he could to get away. I never saw this behavior at any other time with Mr. Cool, but it was repeated throughout his life with every veterinarian I took him to see. I could almost see the mental picture he put out of being in a cage where experiments were carried out on him by men in white lab coats. How else can you explain this type of behavior except past life experiences?

German Shepherds come equipped with instincts that are meant for survival in the wild. Not all of these impulses are advantageous to a dog or you in a home setting.

If in your interactions you treat a puppy with respect and firm resolve in your interactions he will quickly bond with you. Karnak decided to make a powerful and unbreakable bond with me in less than a month. It was impossible for me not to return the feeling. This doesn't mean that he obeyed my every command or request, but it formed the basis from which a great relationship was created.

The effective ingredient of all training with German Shepherds puppies is repetition and consistency. You must be consistent. There used to be an expression to describe a method of teaching called "Chinese School". I assume the derivation of the term came from its use in schools in China in the early 20th century. It simply meant that the teacher would stand at the head of the class and say something and the students would repeat it and the teacher would say it again, and the students would repeat it until it stuck with the students. If you use this teaching method by showing and telling what you want your dog to learn it will eventually sink in with him. Sometimes it is hard to be consistent but this is very important. If you selectively enforce rules, the dog may never adhere to them. Many is the time when you will be sitting down, or eating, or on the phone and you will see the puppy doing something it shouldn't. It seems like so much effort to get up and correct the pooch, but you should. Repetition and Consistency are key.

When you speak to your Shepherd, do not use baby talk. Speak to him in normal English or whatever your language is. If you use baby talk you will get a baby. German Shepherds do not fully mature until they are two and a half to three years old. Their brains are growing when they are puppies. They grow so fast when they are young that every week you can see their skulls get bigger and their bodies stretching out. Intelligent handling encourages and stimulates brain development in areas that will allow them to master more complex subjects as they mature.

When you take a puppy home you have to realize that he is being torn away from his dog family and everything he knows. So of course there is a period of adjustment. It is very important to make the puppy feel safe in his new home. You cannot expect him to immediately accept your home as comfortable and secure. You need a little patience here.

When I bought Karnak home the first night he wanted to sleep as far away from me as he could get. I let him sleep where he wanted. Each night he would pick a spot closer and closer to me. Soon he wanted to sleep at my feet, but it took a week or two. Once he felt more secure, I made him sleep in the wire enclosure within sight of me. When I wanted Karnak to go with me outside, at first he was very cautious. For a car trip I had to pick him up and carry him to the car, but after a number of times he readily would come on his own volition.

This brings up a very important quality needed in the human: PATIENCE. Here is the definition of the word: "the quality of being patient, as the bearing of provocation, annoyance, misfortune, or pain, without complaint, loss of temper, or the like." Puppies will, at times, ignore you, act wildly, and generally create chaos. You must not give into your lower impulses. Often I have put Karnak outside for a time-out when he was out of control, but I never became impatient or acted irrationally toward him. This is not always easy to do, but it is very important to your dog's upbringing.

Petting your puppy. Pets should be handed out liberally and often. A good pet works both ways. Petting makes the dog feel good and also makes the owner feel good. Spend as much time as you can with your pooch. I do not care for a dog tongue on my face or lips. I have seen where those canine tongues have gone where no man should. I have always taught my pets to accept air kisses. As a child I had the most wonderful grandmother, but she had one most unappealing habit. She always thought she should kiss you on the lips for hello and goodbye. She had a little mustache, and maybe I have never recovered from feeling that stash, but not kissing your dog is better for sanitation. No tongue touching my face. Dogs get used to this and after a while accept air kisses as quite satisfactory. That way the pooch does not feel his show of affection is being rejected, and you won't feel like you need to cleanse your lips.

German Shepherds and many other dogs have a great sense of time. Since they cannot read a clock, I cannot explain how they know when it is time for a walk or to eat, etc., but they do. The best way is to adhere to a schedule for feeding or other regular activities. Predictability is calming for a puppy and helps a dog learn your expectations of him. This ties in with consistency. Order appeals to a puppy as it does to a sane human. Sane beings basically feel more comfortable with order rather than chaos, so do German Shepherds.

At the root of every problem is chaos and unpredictability. A problem is being caught between yes and no, go or stay, this creates a maybe or confusion. Selecting one or the other resolves the problem. Predictability avoids a confusion. I am not talking about complete rigidity of routine, but general orderliness is appealing. When there is going to be a change to routine, just tell the puppy first. They may not understand every word you are saying, but they will get the general idea and be calmed by your communication. German shepherds have the inclination to bring order into disorder, encourage this.

I am amused when on occasion I read some article that reports scientists at some university have studied dogs for the last 10 years and spent millions of dollars to come to a conclusion like "yes dogs can recognize and make a selection between two different toys". For heaven's sake, just open your eyes! Adult German Shepherds make a hundred decisions each day. It is easy to observe that they approach (resolve) similar problems in a similar way. Their actions are not based on some random popcorn machine basis or always the same robotic action. Just watch your Shepherd on any day, he will clearly make decisions from his viewpoint of optimum survival in a logical fashion. Humans are so caught up in their own world that they often can't seem to recognize that survival decisions (the effort to stay in this space and time) are the most basic urge or impetus behind decisions for all life forms, but they are not always the same for dogs as for humans.

Puppies constantly want your attention and involvement with them. Sometimes this gets to be too much. I find one of the most useful of commands to be: "Play by Yourself" sometimes with a waving away of the hand. Eventually the puppy will get this; by the time he matures he will understand and obey this. A very practical command. Remember to let the puppy have fun, his fun may not always be what you consider to be fun, but you need to work it out.

All humans do not learn or absorb information at the same pace; neither do canines. It is important in teaching a dog concepts that you remain patient and persistent. The principle of 'gradients' always applies to learning for humans or dogs. Break the concept down into sub-concepts until he gets it. Until the previous idea is grasped, do not move onto the next one. Neither humans nor dogs can jump to the top of the ladder without first navigating the lower steps. (Doctor once actually climbed up a ladder to join me on the roof, after that I pulled the ladder up behind me). There are lots of text books that do not logically explain the lower rungs before jumping to the higher ones. This just makes learning difficult. A puppy needs to understand "come" before you let him run off on his own. In proper and graspable increments most anything can be learned.

One of the troubles with our educational system is that the machine of schooling keeps moving ahead with more concepts no matter whether the student has understood and comprehended the last idea. This creates a chronic condition for many students where not understanding the previous concept distorts the next related idea.

When I brought Karnak home, one of the first lessons I wanted him to learn was to lie down. For some reason I didn't have to say "lie down" (accompanied with a hand gesture indicating down) more than a few times. He also immediately got "Come Here" and "Go in your Box" (box was my expression for his exercise pen). In my experience "Stay" is the most difficult concept to get a puppy to obey and I am still working on that one with Karnak. Be persistent in your instructions and one day, usually just about when you are ready to give up, he will obey. It would be foolish not to grasp that there are some instructions that the puppy really does understand, but doesn't want to obey. As he becomes comfortable that you are interested in his welfare, he will eventually obey commands he once thought were against his interest.

Most dog training is just hard repetition. Never appealing to the dog's intelligence, just trying to create a stimulus-response. This may be fine for training in bomb sniffing, but when all of the inflow a dog receives is only of this type, it diminishes his ability to discern. This kind of training validates and strengthens the natural ability of the dog Being and his body cells to copy and duplicate and makes an impression on his being and cells, but will take away his judgment as the memories and cell impressions overwhelm the basic personality of the Being.

The same is true in humans most of whom are buried under huge amounts of mental and bodily impulses from their past that can overwhelm a Being's innate logic, order, and ability to decide issues on the environment before them rather than on some past events not now present.

You want your companion to have judgement not just automatic responses to situations. German Shepherds are capable of judgment. Here is the definition of that word: the ability to judge, make a decision, or form an opinion objectively, authoritatively, and wisely, especially in matters affecting action; with good sense; discretion.

I am not suggesting that we turn matters of war and peace over to the dogs although in some recent cases perhaps they could not have made worse decisions than our human political leaders who have sent our people and dogs into war zones for no benefit. The steadfastness of a German Shepherd is a quality of which Winston Churchill would have been proud, but I digress.... My point is that in matters that occur in the life of a German shepherd it is better to appeal to judgment learned along with their unwavering loyalty to humans than to just let them be wild non-thinking dogs. When you appeal to the body or stimulus-response only, you can submerge the being.

Socialization is very important to a puppy. The first socialization he gets will be from you and your family. All should treat the puppy with respect. The more situations a dog is exposed to as a puppy, the more confident he will be as an adult.

Walks are very good for puppy and adult GSDs. Unless you live on a farm or ranch, all walks for a puppy must be done on leash. German Shepherds are curious by nature and love to check out the local smells. For a GSD a walk is like an opportunity to catch up on the local news. It is like reading the newspaper or a website of local sightings of dog friends and enemies which they do thru their sense of smell, perhaps it could be known as The Smelly Times or The Smeller Post. Remember dogs don't read on the internet but rather thru their noses. I like to conduct the walk for their benefit, letting them go to different smells and leave their mark for the next dog.

A walk gives your dog an opportunity to mark his territory and cover up the markings of dogs previously there. This is normal German Shepherd communication. In a way a dog is leaving a warning to others to stay out of the territory he is protecting. When you think it through he is laying down a protection marker to keep other animals away from his family which includes you. No one knows for sure but I think that dogs assume humans can smell too, and are leaving a mark for all trespassers. German Shepherds are aggressive markers on walks and this is all part of their protection of their human family. A walk also is an opportunity for a dog to interact with other humans, sounds, sights, and other dogs.

I do not like dog parks for German Shepherds unless you know all the other dogs present. I once took Dante to a very large dog park. We were minding our own business when two rather large Rottweilers ran up and tried to pick a fight with Dante. Some owners do not pay attention or take proper care of their animals at such venues. You can never be sure what will happen when your dog meets up with another canine for the first time, so be cautious and keep the leash tight. After all, who can say for sure what will happen when two humans meet?

When I see people running or biking with their dogs in tow, I know that the dog is not getting the most out of the walk. Maybe he is getting some exercise, but it steals away the dog's natural instinct to catch up on local activity and leave his mark on the world. Such a walk robs him of his desire to self-determine his way in the world. When you blunt self-determination you get acting out and craziness.

Most humans and dogs are other-determined and driven with compulsions and inhibitions stemming from their minds and bodies. Observing agreements is necessary for a civilized society, but taking away all self–determinism does not make a happy human or a happy dog.

Time to speak of the word "No" or for the German purists "Nein". Expect to use this word or equivalents a lot during the puppy phase. There is no way around it. Puppies will continually test you over and over and often just do things without thinking. You need to correct them or they will never learn. Validation of good behavior is even more important. When they are behaving correctly or just doing what is civilized I often tell Karnak "good boy", or "good work", or my personal favorite "good pooching". The exact words of affirmation are not as important as the tone and intention behind the words, and your dog will quickly come to understand praise in any form. We are often quick to criticize but much slower to praise good work. You will get more of what you validate in humans or canines. The only people who get excessive undeserved validation are celebrities.

A smart German Shepherd sees you as his partner. They are willing to let you have the last word once they see your leadership qualities. Having a partnership for life is very important to a Shepherd. If you are good to them, they will never ask for a divorce or desert you. How many humans can you count on for this same loyalty? Shepherds are also very forgiving. Even after a disagreement, they will greet you enthusiastically.

There is no better greeting than a tail wagging German Shepherd. When you arrive home a Shepherd will exhibit pleasure and excitement at your arrival. In turn, you will derive pleasure from their enthusiasm. Shepherds have a full and strong tail which they crank up to maximum speed and velocity when they are happy. If I were king I would require that all humans have tails. Wouldn't it be nice to know what another person felt about you? Tails would bring out a level of honesty in discourse that would probably shame most politicians. The world sorely needs this honesty.

A greeting from your German Shepherd when you come in the door brightens everything. There is no better welcome in the whole wide world. I have seen some breeds of dogs be covert. In my experience a well-treated German Shepherd is incapable of insincerity.

A Shepherd has great patience and tolerance for man, and he will put up with a lot of illogic without complaint; so, in turn, you as a human should have great patience and tolerance for puppy behavior. This is not always easy. I placate myself with the knowledge that the puppy period does not last forever. Try to keep this in mind when your puppy has gotten ahold of a roll of toilet paper and torn it up all over the house. When Mr. Cool was a puppy he loved to go into the bathroom off the main bedroom and grab ahold of the end of the roll, and unroll it all the way out of the bathroom, thru the bedroom, and into the living room where I was working. After the third time of cleaning this up, it occurred to me I just needed to shut the door to the bedroom. Karnak has already shown a penchant for chewing on toilette paper rolls.

Often solutions to combat bad puppy behavior are easy if you just stop and think for a minute. The best way to avoid having your puppy destroy your possessions is to block his access or put them up higher than his reach. Keep in mind that with his rapid rate of growth what he can't reach today, he may be able to reach by next week.

German Shepherds grow at an amazing rate. Of course while all this is happening they also have hormones flowing in their bodies. Much going on to stimulate a puppy into action. This may account in part for why one moment the puppy will be running all over the place and at another time will be calm. Unless you beat a puppy into submission which you should never do, they will all have idiosyncrasies just like humans do. German Shepherds are not rote completely programmable machines. As you do with your human friends and family you must accept this, in turn, your pooch will accept you.

Karnak gave what I would call his first real bark at four months. At four and a half months he is already keeping watch over the back yard. I see him looking out even beyond the fence ready to warn off any intruding animals or people.

I have often gone away for the summer, and immediately my dogs adapted to the new environment and guarded the perimeter of the new property. Shepherds care about their friends not material things. For a Shepherd, home is wherever his owner is.

By now you should be getting the idea of how unique and special German Shepherds are. You should have also figured out that they are not for everyone. To provide a proper home for a GSD it takes a caring and aware individual as well as someone who will spend time with their pooch. If you are that type of person, the rewards are bountiful.

A good general reference site is the German Shepherd Guide[9]

---

[9] http://www.germanshepherdguide.com/

Mr. Cool on walk at San Simeon Point

Mr. Cool, the puppy and his trail of toilette paper

Mr. Cool relaxing in meadow in Colorado mountains

Mr. Cool in Uncompahgre National Forest

Mr. Cool exploring on walk in Colorado mountains

Mr. Cool in back yard at home

Mr. Cool lounging on deck

Mr. Cool in back of SUV

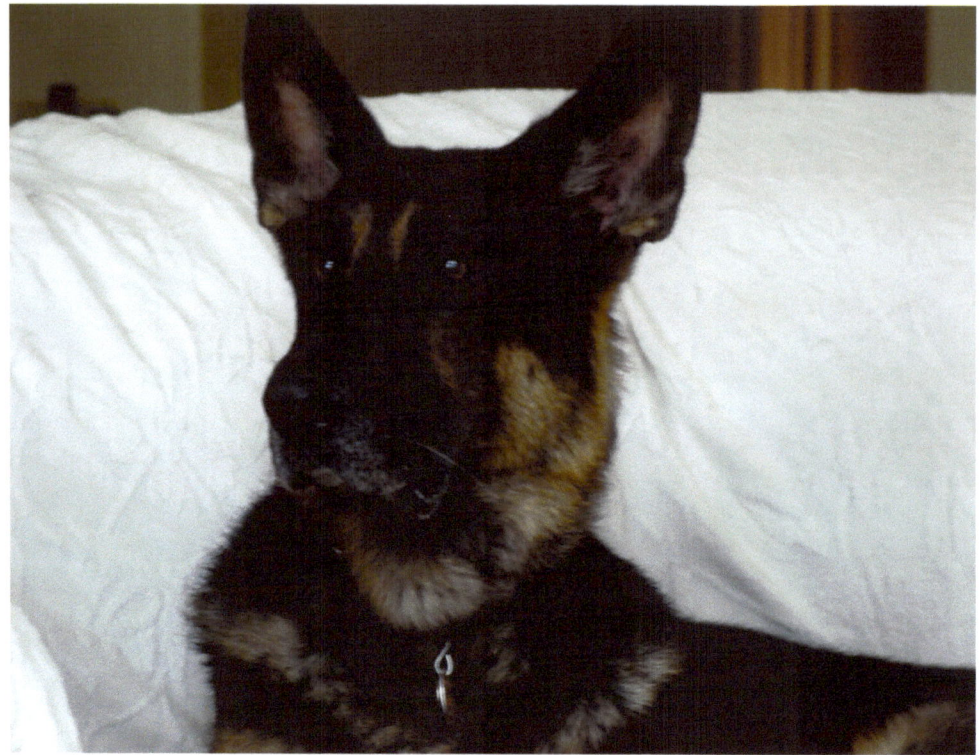
Mr. Cool at 10 years old

Mr. Cool and mail man – used this as holiday card with caption: Peace on Earth

EPILOGUE

Mr. Cool always wished to go in the car with me, and when I went shopping I often let him come with me. When I would return to my car which was an SUV with a split tail gate, and I opened the top portion of the gate to put the groceries in the car, Mr. Cool would immediately stick his head out to check out the surroundings.

Maybe once every two or three weeks someone walking by would stop and say something about how much he or she really missed their Shepherd, or they asked could they pet Mr. Cool, or they would want to tell me about their Shepherd. Sometimes these people would look very affluent, sometimes middle class, sometimes blue collar working people, and sometimes very scruffy. Whatever their standing in this life when they spoke of their Shepherds their tone would rise, and a look of happiness would be quite visible on their faces. I would gladly stop and converse with them. Afterwards, I would always feel heartened and lifted in spirit for hours. I can't think of any other topic that will always makes me feel this way. In fact, I probably would never have spoken a word to these people in the parking lot under other circumstances; yet, for hours afterwards I too felt uplifted.

It is hard to find words that are adequate to describe what having the companionship of a great German Shepherd has meant to me. They have so many traits that appeal to me at my very core.

Shepherds are imbued with an abundance of alertness, acute intelligence, communication skills, courage, independence, curiosity, tenacity, a full range of emotions, sincerity, capability for logical reasoned judgment, self-confidence, persistence, fearlessness, a great sense of play, a quick ability to learn, a bond with their owner that cannot be broken, a desire to work, fantastic physical abilities, enthusiasm, and great caring for their owners.

Sometimes it is rough and tumble in the world of GSDs, but in the end you can always count on them for their steadfastness to you.

Generally humans are so overwhelmed and battered by the ardors and stresses of everyday living that they forgo many of these principles. Perhaps Shepherds could provide a good lesson for our children.

Most people overlook the importance of great character traits. Schools don't really teach them. One or two stories about George Washington and the cherry tree and the world moves on to 'every man for himself'. Doesn't this lead to wars, pain, suffering, and class warfare?

With our nation more divided than ever, can we not take a lesson from our German Shepherd pals. They are afraid of almost nothing and stand up for their human friends without bullying or extorting their neighborhood. If they must do battle, once the fight is over they hold no grudge.

Of course they are dogs, and cannot reason with the full powers of a human, but if humans were to adopt a German Shepherd's living philosophy, the lot of man would be far improved.

What if humans were focused on carrying on the traits of a GSD?

Intelligence: How many humans work at improving their capacity for learning and understanding?

Alertness: How many of us go through the day not really paying attention to our surroundings and how the people around us are doing?

Communication skills: Don't most people just throw out some words, never- minding to see if their ideas were clearly received?

Courage: Do most people put courage behind their convictions?

Independence: Aren't most people content to go along with the majority whether they agree or not?

Curiosity: How many just want to get the day over and get home to an alcoholic beverage rather than explore new vistas?

Tenacity: Don't many just give up on their goals when opposition appears?

Sincerity: Couldn't we use a lot more of this in our lives?

Capability for logical reasoned judgment: Don't we need more of this?

Self-confidence: Who amongst us doesn't have self-doubt?

Persistence: Do you always make it through to your goal?

Fearlessness: Do you know anyone who is always fearless?

A great sense of play: How many really enjoy their entire day?

A quick ability to learn: As people get older aren't they less interested in learning?

A bond with their loved ones: Look at the divorce rate.

A desire to work: How productive are most people?

Fantastic physical abilities: How many infirmed are there in the world?

Enthusiasm: Where is all the genuine enthusiasm?

Great Caring for their owners: Don't we need more love?

There are no perfect conditions on earth, but moving forward in life with the above attributes would be a step in the right direction. We can learn much and enjoy much from the life style of a German Shepherd Dog.

Maybe there would be no wars if everyone responsibly owned a German Shepherd, certainly there would be more kindness and love.

Karnak at three months

A young Karnak

Karnak in Colorado mountains on one of his first outings

Young Karnak

Karnak in car. He liked to ride in the shotgun seat

Karnak having laugh in car

Karnak in his exercise pen

Karnak at home in living room

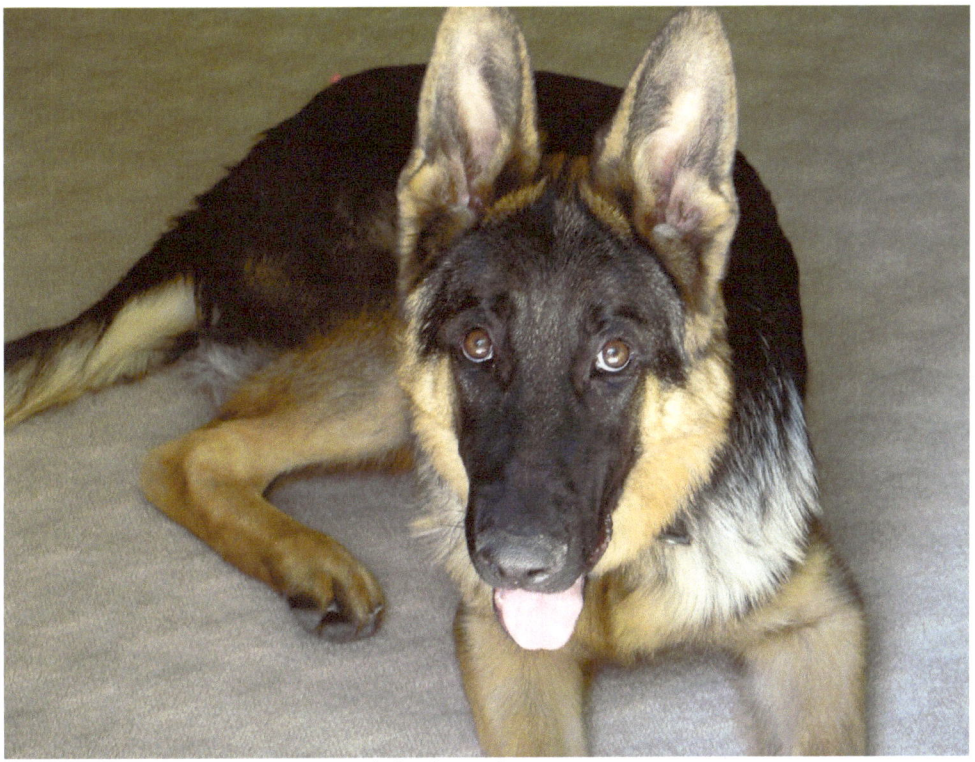
Karnak looking for some action

Karnak in back yard at 5 months of age

ABOUT THE AUTHOR

THE AUTHOR, ANDREW P POLLACK, HAS ENJOYED LIVING CHEEK TO JOWL WITH GERMAN SHEPHERDS FOR THE LAST 45 YEARS.

HE IS A MASTER OUT DOOR PHOTOGRAPHER AND HAS FOR DECADES PHOTOTGRAPHED MOUNTAIN AND OCEAN SCENARY IN THE WESTERN UNITED STATES.

SOME OF HIS PHOTOGRAPHY CAN BE SEEN ON HIS FACEBOOK PAGE.

www.ingramcontent.com/pod-product-compliance
Lightning Source LLC
Chambersburg PA
CBHW061047090426
42740CB00002B/72